AF559647

The Adventures of SUPER DIAPER BABY

The First Graphic Novel

Written and illustrated by DAV PILKEY
as George Beard and Harold Hutchins
with color by Wes Dzioba

An imprint of
SCHOLASTIC

For my mom and dad — G.R.B.
To Mom and Heidi — H.M.H.

Library of Congress Control Number 2024950266

ISBN 978-93-5954-627-8

Printed and boundin India by Thomson Press India Private Limited
First color edition printing, August 2025
This color edition reprint, February 2026

Editorial team: Ken Geist and Jonah Newman
Book design by Dav Pilkey, Phil Falco, and Jooahn Kwon
Color by Wes Dzioba
Creative Director: Phil Falco
Publisher: David Saylor

The ORIGIN of Super Diaper Baby

An introduction by
George Beard and Harold Hutchins

Once upon a time there were two cool kids named George and Harold.

One time they were in the gym running over ketchup packs on their skateboards.

It was fun until their mean principal, Mr. Krupp, came by.

Hey!

Clean up this Mess!

When you're done, meet me in my office, bubs!

Normally I would make you write sentences For a punishment... but that doesn't teach You anything!

So instead I'm Going to make you write A 100-page essay on "Good Citizenship."

And I don't want you kids turning in a 100-page comic Book About "Captain Underpants," either! That is UNACCEPT-able.

Aw man.

no Fair.

George and Harold were Bummed.

Then They got a great idea!

So they went home and got to work.

The next day they turned in their 100-Page "essay."

... AND SO...

I will not make offensive comic books.
I will not make offensive comic books.
I will not make offensive comic books.
I will

I will not make offensive comic
I will not make offensive comic
I will not make offensive comic
I will not make

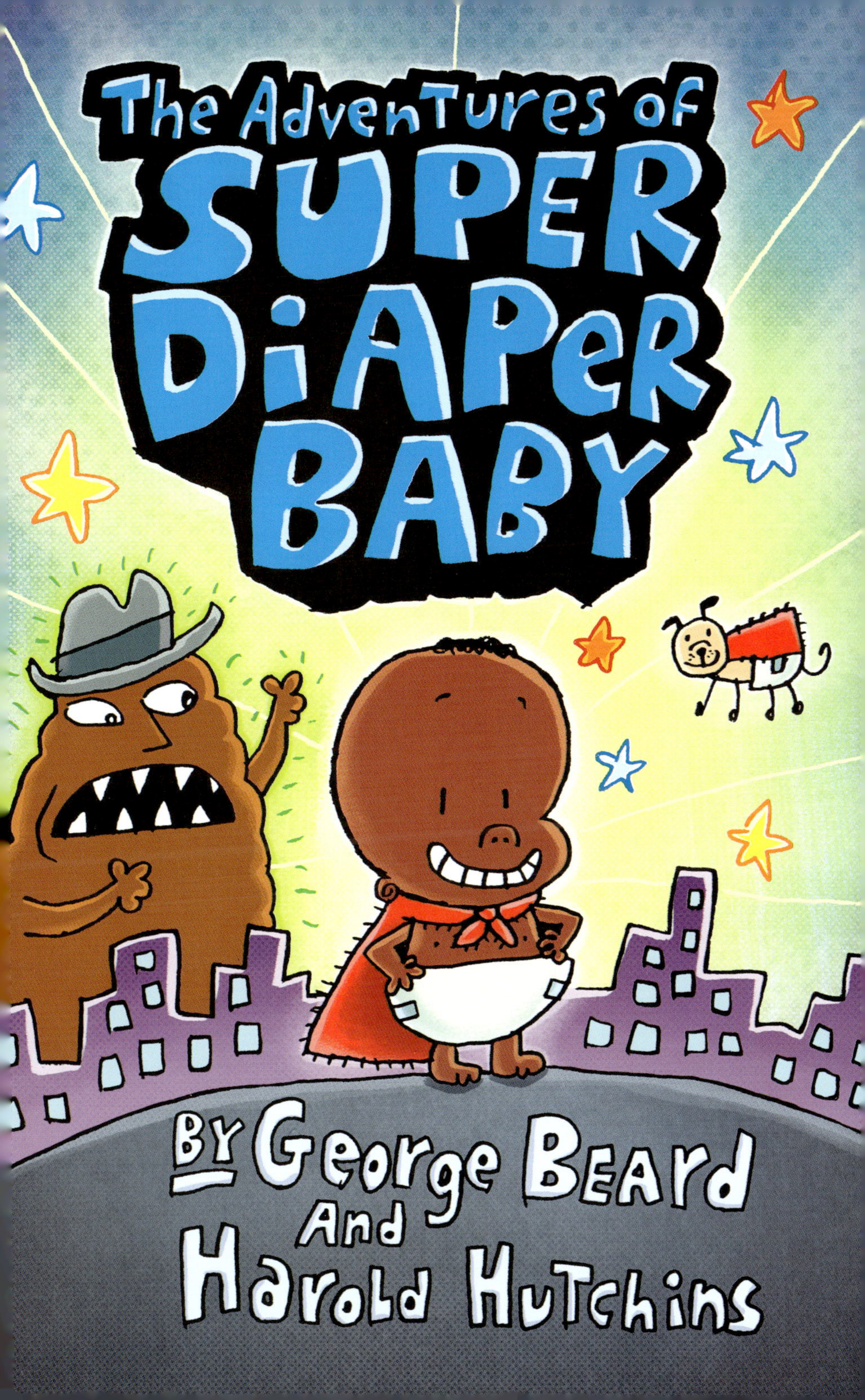

The Adventures of SUPER DIAPER BABY

By George Beard And Harold Hutchins

Chapters

The Adventures of SUPER DIAPER BABY

Our story Begins as a car is speeding to the Hospital.
Hurry up!
I'm Hurry upping!

HOSPITAL
SCREECH

Come on!
O.K.

Nurse- we're going to Have a baby!
Me too!

Alright, but First you HAVE to Answer some Questions.
O.K.

Name?
Gosh, we Haven't Picked out a name YeT.

NOT The Baby's Name! YOUR Name!
OH! BiLL and Mary Hoskins.

AGe?
Gee, I Guess He will be zero.

NOT The BAby's Age!!! Your AGe!
OH. 30 and a half.

OCCU-PATion?
well He won't Be old enough For A JoB Just yeT.

OH FOR CRYinG OUT LOUD!

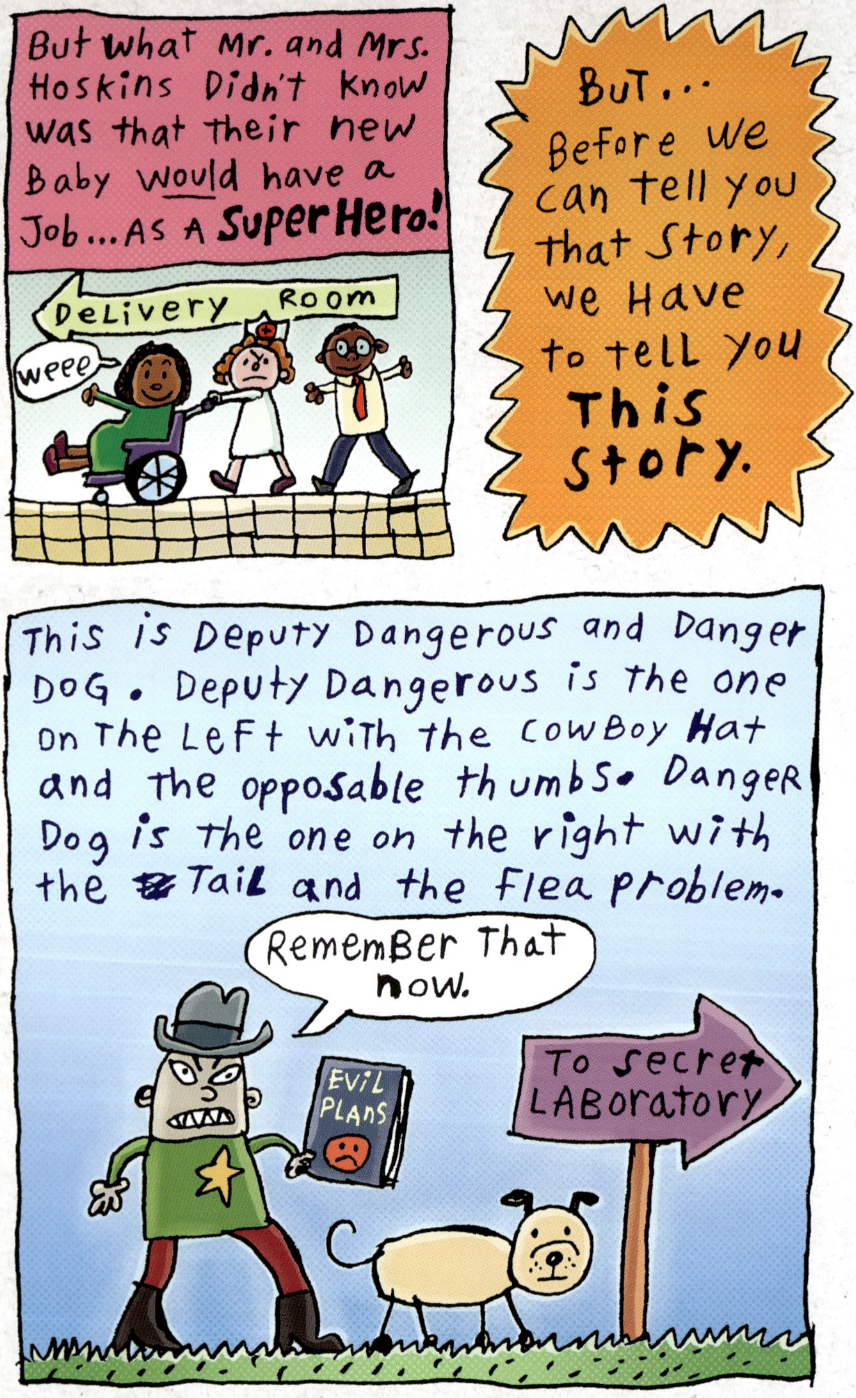

But...
Before we can tell you that Story, we Have to tell you **This Story.**

This is Deputy Dangerous and Danger Dog. Deputy Dangerous is the one on The Left with the cowBoy Hat and the opposable thumbs. Danger Dog is the one on the right with the Tail and the Flea problem.

Remember That now.

Evil Plans

To Secret LABoratory

Deputy Dangerous was mean and Ruth-Less.
I am evil, too.

Danger Dog was also bad, too.
I'm not really evil. I'm Just in it for The Kibbles.
Hey!

Together they opened up an Underwear Laundry. But it was a TRAP!
YE OLde Underwear CLEANERS
underwear cleaned while you wait
Super-Heroes Welcome

Soon came the moment that Deputy Dangerous was waiting for.
Tra-La-Laaaa!
YE OLde Under
CLEAN
Look who's Here! It's Captain Underpants!
My Hero!

Hi, captain. Would you like to try our Super-Deluxe cleaning for free?

O.K.

What HAppened? I- I- I Feel so weak.
That's Because I took Your Powers Away. Haw Haw Haw!

Behold: Your Super-powers were Trans-formed into This Juice.

ALL we Have to do is drink this Superpower Juice And we will get Superpowers!
COOL!

You drink HALF then I'LL drink HALF. Then we will RULE The World.
O.K.
GLUB GLUB Glub

KA-POW

Hey Look at me! I can FLY!!!

Now I will drink the rest of the Superpower Juice.

CRASH
COPS

We heard Somebody Fire an iLLegal "Super Power Taker-Awayer 2000".
COPS
COPS

Now hold it Right there, cowboy!
Save me, cops!
OH NO!
COPS
COPS

Let's Get out of Here, Danger DoG.
OK, why not?

Danger Dog used His new Laser eye powers to Burn A hole in The WALL.
ZAP

Hey, they escaped!
COPS
COPS
Rats.
So Long, Losers!
ZIP

So Deputy Dangerous rode on his Flying dog through the city with the cops in hot pursuit.
Hey, Come Back Here!
YeeHAW!

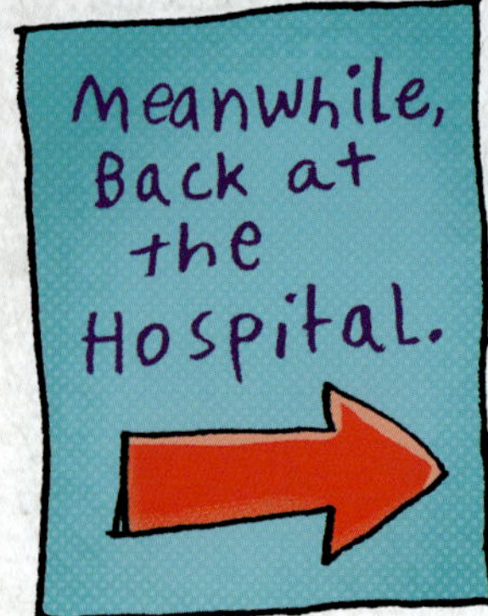
Meanwhile,
Back at
the
Hospital.

PUSH!

POP

Congratulations! You got a Baby Boy.

Now I have to Give him the "spank of Life."
Aw man, can't you Just give him a time-out?

No way. It's a tradition. ALL doctors do this.
A-one and A-TWO And A...

...Three.
oops... sorry!
SMACK
CRASH

LOOK What YOU Did!
MY BABY!
Hey, I said I was sorry. Geez!

At that very Moment, Deputy Dangerous and Super Danger Dog were Flying By.
HOS-PIT-AL
Stop!

Haw Haw Haw!

SPLASH

GLUB
GLUB
GLUB
GLUB
GLUB
GLUB
what the-

KA·POW

Hey, You lousy Baby! You drank all my Super-Power Juice! —Give it to Me NOW!!!

WARNING

THE Following pages contains scenes showing A baby teaching a bad guy some Respect!!! Get ready to be offended.....

Graphic violins

HERE'S HOW IT WORKS!!!!

STEP 1
Place your left hand inside the dotted lines marked "LEFT HAND HERE." Hold the book open FLAT.

STEP 2
Grasp the right-hand page with your right thumb and index finger (inside the dotted lines marked "RIGHT THUMB HERE").

STEP 3
Now quickly flip the right-hand page back and forth until the picture appears to be animated!

(for extra fun, try adding your own sound-effects)

FLIP-O-RAMA # 1

(Pages 25 and 27)

Remember, flip only page 25. While you are flipping, be sure you can see the picture on page 25 And the one on page 27.

If you flip quickly, the two pictures will start to look like one animated picture.

Don't forget to add your own sound-effects!

Left hand here.

Take this!

Take this!

FLIP-O-RAMA # 2

(pages 29 and 31)

Remember, flip *only* page 29. While you are flipping, be sure you can see the picture on page 29 *And* the one on page 31.

If you flip quickly, the two pictures will start to look like *one* Animated picture.

Don't forget to add your own sound-effects!

Left hand here.

... And that!

... And that!

FLIP-O-RAMA #3

(pages 33 and 35)

Remember, Flip only page 33. While you are flipping, be sure you can see the picture on page 33 and page 35.

If you flip quickly, the two pictures will start to look like yadda yadda yadda.

Don't forget to skip these pages without reading them.

Left hand here.

...And some of these!

... And some of these!

WOW- That baby stopped A CROOK! He's A Hero!
Doggy.

I'm A nurse! I'm A nurse!
COPS
COPS
SQUISH

Are you O.K., Little BAby?
DOGGY.
SQUASH

I'm putting a Diaper on you.
SNIFF
SNIFF

Now Let's go up-stairs to see your mommy and daddy.
Momma.
DAddy.

And so Super Diaper Baby Flew up and was Reunited with his mom and Dad.
HOS-PiT-AL
Gee, You don't see that every day.
COPS
COPS

Left hand here.

ALL is Forgiven

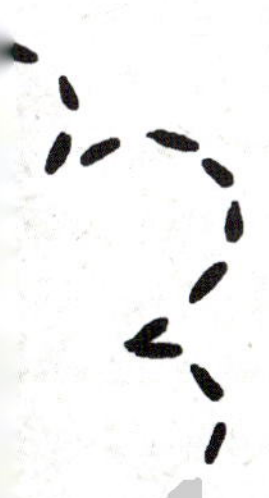

ALL is Forgiven

So Mr. and Mrs. Hoskins took their new Baby "BiLLy" home from the hospital.

SUPER DI-APER BABY

Chapter 2
The Evil Plan

Deputy Dangerous and Danger Dog went straight to jail. But they escaped.
City Jail for Bad guys and dogs.
CRASH
I'm free!
Hey!

Then they flew to a secret Laboratory high on a mountain.
weeee!
secret LABoratory

Now I will invent an invention to Get Revenge!!!
Knock Yourself out!

So Deputy Dangerous worked all night on the Danger-CRIB 2000!™
z z z z z z

Lookit! I made a crib that will transfer all of that baby's super-powers to me!

Now we must deliver this crib to the Hoskinses.
What crib?

Pay attention next time!
The Hoskinses
DinG Dong
huh?

can I help you?
Hi. my name is Deputy um... "Undangerous." And This is um... "SAFeTy Dog."
THE Hoskinses
How's it Going?

You just won this free crib for your new baby!

Gee, Thanks. You Guys rule!
Bye-Bye.

That night

Good night, Billy.
Sleep good in your new crib.

Meanwhile, back at the secret lab...
Transfer Helmet
Haw Haw Haw! It's almost midnight. Soon I will be transformed!

BUT

At 11:59 P.M., something unexpected happened.
MOMMA!

What is it, honey?
me Pooped.

That's OK. We'LL Leave Your Poopy diaper in the crib And I will give You A nice Bath.

RRRRRR

ZAP

Where did Poopy Go?
I don't Know, BiLLy. It's Gone!
SSSSSS

But at that very moment, The Poop was Being Beamed to a satellite.

SATELLITE

ZING

ZAP

?
TRANSFER
Helmet

Hey, what happened?
TRANSFER
Helmet

I- I don't feel any stronger.
You sure SMELL stronger, Bub!
sniff
sniff

Hey, How'd you get so BiG?
I Think you better Look in This mirror.

what the...
what the...
I'm a Piece of Poo!
He's a Piece of Poo!

ReLax--- it could be worse.
I GoT Turned into POOP!!! How could This be any worse?

You could have been Turned into diarrhea.
OH Be QuieT!

Left hand here.

---Aw Maaaaaan!!!

---Aw Maaaaaan!!!

Aw Man! I stepped in an evil villian!
Don't you Hate when that happens?

SCRAPE

Stupid DOG.
Oh, Right! Blame the dog!
Trash

Hey Deputy... are you O.K.?
Trash

MUST...
Trash

...Get...
Trash

...RevenGE!
Trash

SUPER DiAPER BABY

CHAPTER 3

Dial "R" For "Revenge"

Boy, this hill is steep! I'm so Tired!
are you pooped?

Why yes, I'm... Hey! Be Quiet!

Aw, don't be a Party Pooper!

I SAID Be Quiet!!!

When we get home will you read me "Winnie the Pooh"?

STOP!

When they got back to their Laboratory, Deputy Dangerous began making an all-new invention.
Z Z Z Z Z Z

Well, Danger Dog, what do you think of my Robo-Ant 2000?

Can I call you "Deputy Doo-Doo" from now on?

AAAAUGH!

You won't think it's so funny after I destroy the world, bub!
Tee-Hee.

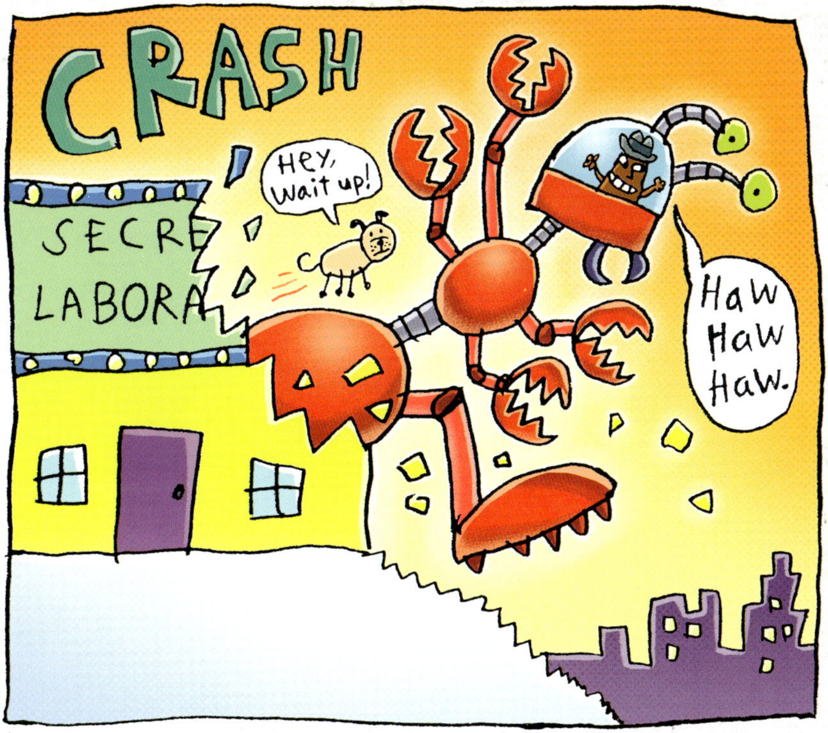

CRASH
SECRE
LABORA
Hey, Wait up!
Haw Haw Haw.

KER-CRAK
It's fun to shop, eat, and drink out at the mall. ALL of the stores have clean Toilets and BIG SALES!

ZAP

It's fun to drink out of the Toilet
Tee-Hee.
It's true, you know!

SAINT Wendy's
HOSPITAL
TRUST in our Great Doctors, Food, And care.

Hi - YAH!!!
CRACK
We SPiT in our FOOD

Bob's Lawn Care
our workers are famous for cutting the weeds and Grass clippings.
Piqua Pizza Palace
Our Pizzas Are made with Fresh
CHEESE

CRACK
CRACK
Bob's Lawn Care
our workers are famous for cutting the
weeds and Grass clippings.
Piqua Pizza Palace
Our Pizzas Are made with Fresh
CHEESE

Switchie switchie!
HEY!
Piqua Pizza Palace
Our Pizzas Are made with Fresh
weeds and Grass clippings.
Bob's Lawn Care
our workers are famous for cutting the
CHEESE

You're supposed to be destroying the world, bub!
I am, Deputy Doo-Doo.

No you're not--- You're just goofing off as usual!
And stop calling me that!
Tee-hee.

Meanwhile, at the Hoskinses' House...
Trash

Mrs. Hoskins was washing dishes when she saw a horrible sight.

Honey, There's a big ant outside The window.
Hee-Hee--- a big ant!

Don't worry, sweetheart. I'LL KiLL the bug for You.

AAAAA-AUGH!

A BUG! A BUG! A BUG!
?

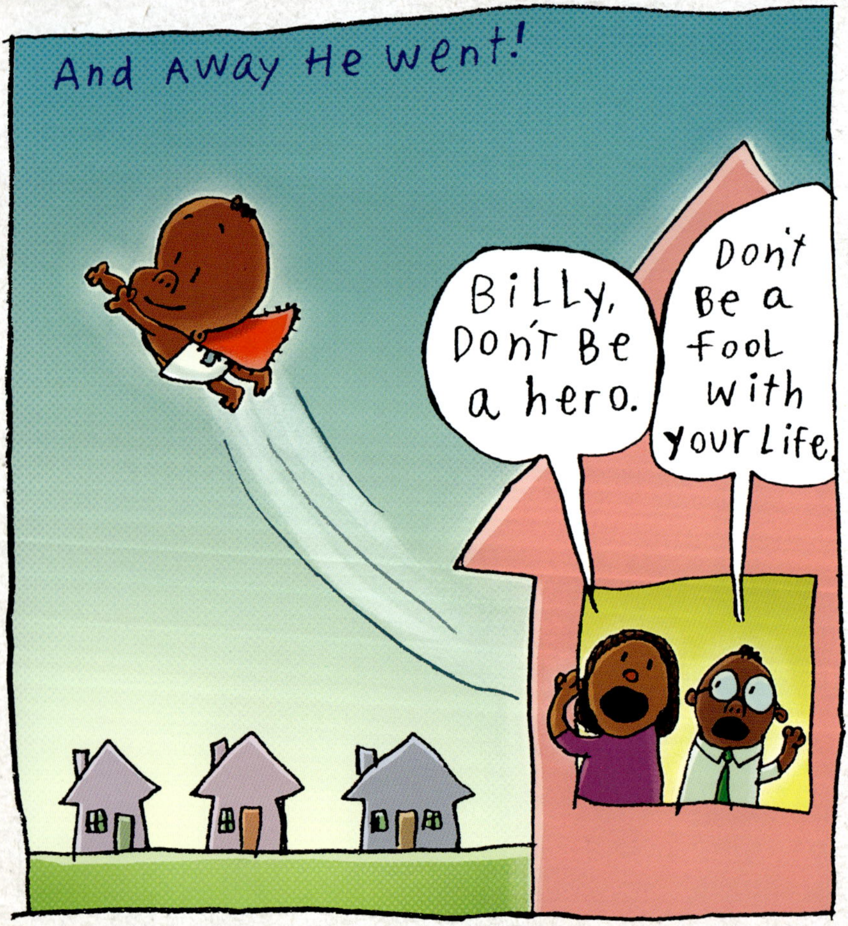

And Away He went!

Billy, Don't Be a hero.

Don't Be a fool with your Life.

Ker-
KrAK

Left hand here.

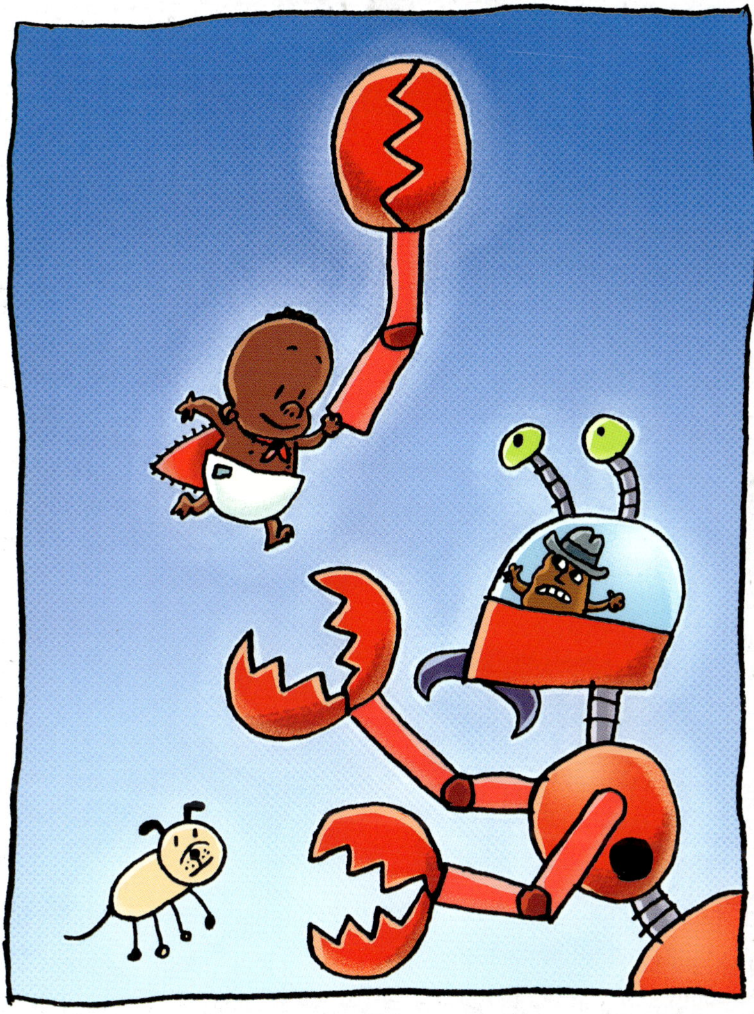

Who's Afraid of the Big, Bad Bug?

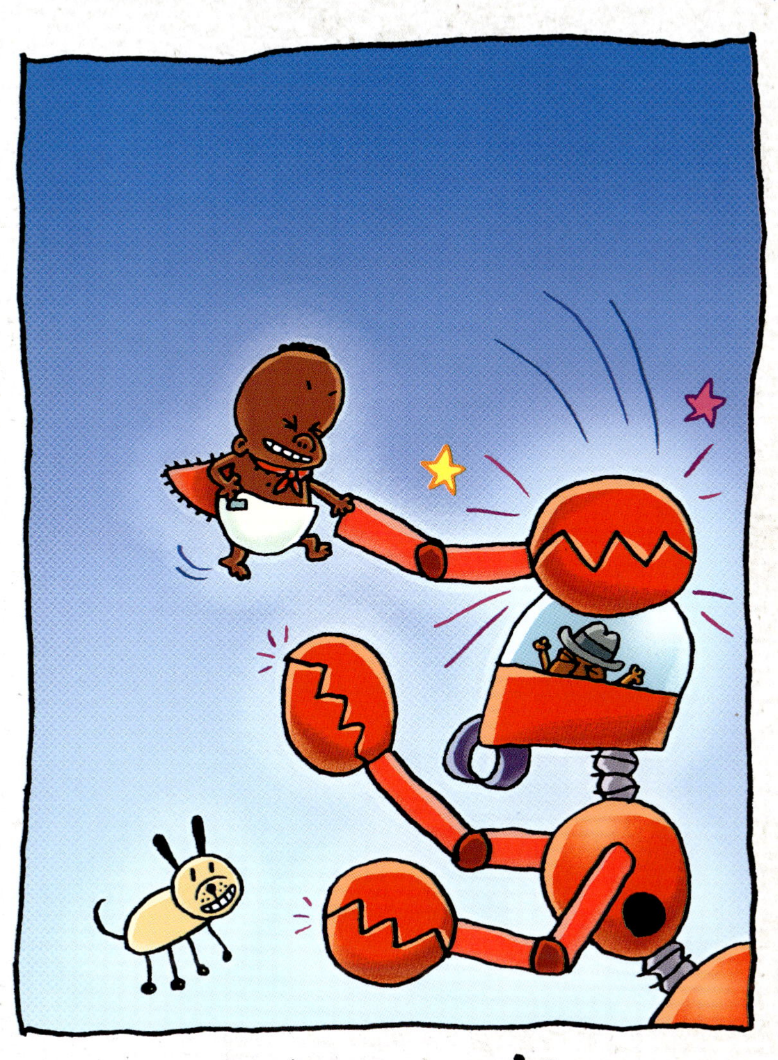

Who's Afraid of the Big, Bad Bug?

FLIP-O-RAMA #7

(pages 73 and 75)

Remember, flip only page 73. While you are flipping, be sure to blah, blah, blah. You're not really reading this page, are you?

Well, since you're here anyway, how about a gross joke? Q: What's the difference between boogers and broccoli?

A: Kids won't eat broccoli.

Left hand here.

ALL Shook up!!!

ALL Shook up!!!

FLIP-O-RAMA #8

(pages **77** and **79**)

Remember, Flip only page 77. So– you're still reading these instructions, eh? Well, how about a Knock-knock Joke?

Knock-knock.

Who's there?

I made up.

I made up, who?

You **DID?** Congratulations!!!

Don't forget to wipe!!!

Left hand here.

Watch out, BiLLy!!!

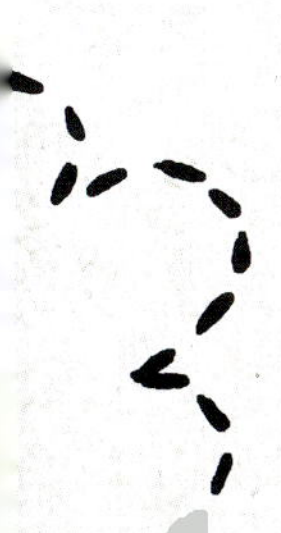

Watch out, Billy!!!

You Crummy BAby!!! You have messed with me for the Last Time!

Hey, He's Just a Kid! Take it easy!!!

No way! If I can't have superpowers, then neither can he!

BuT WAiT.

SUPA NUCLear Power Plant

over 2 Million Mutated

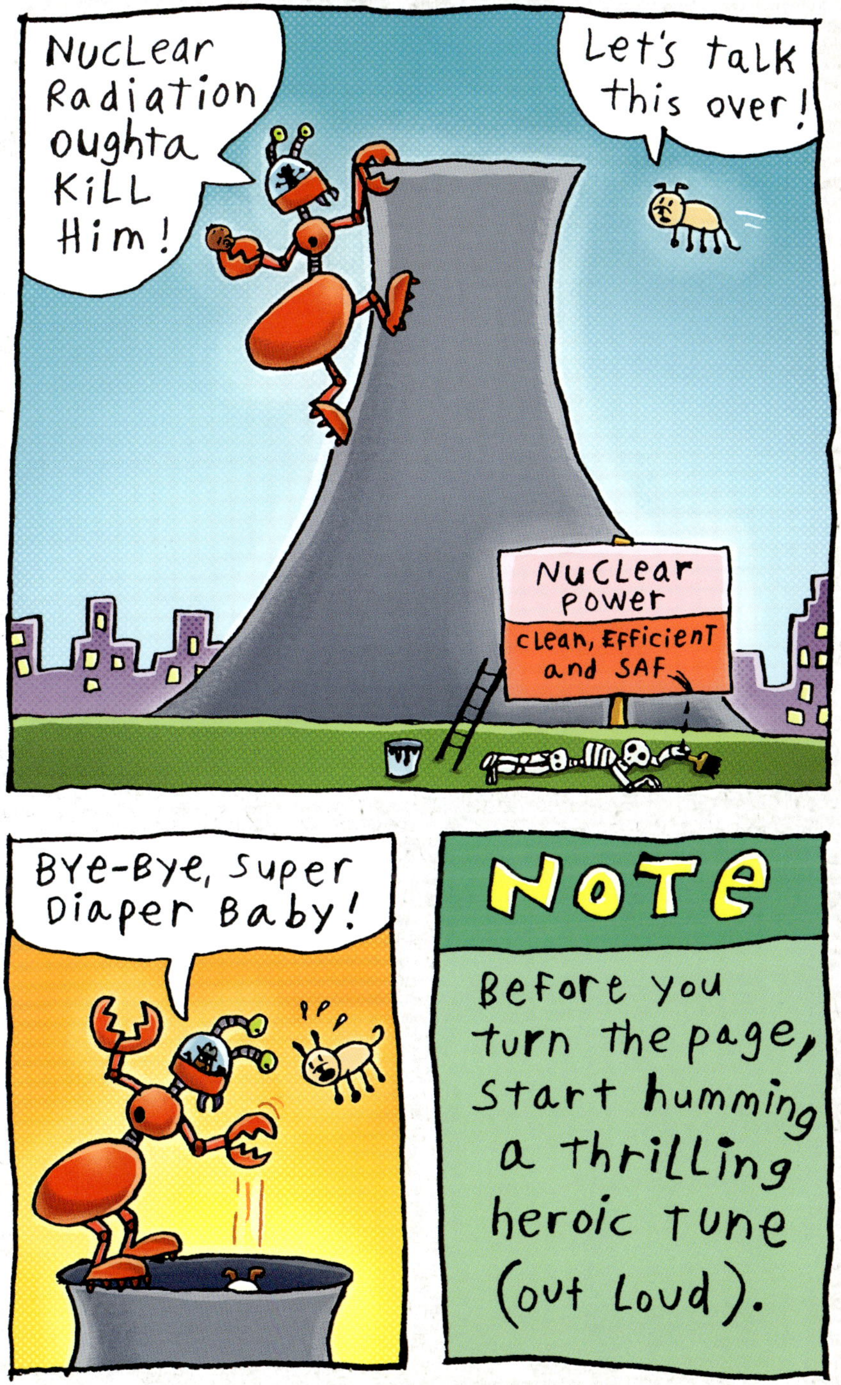

Nuclear Radiation oughta Kill Him!

Let's talk this over!

Nuclear power

clean, Efficient and SAF

NOTE

Before you turn the page, Start humming a thrilling heroic tune (out loud).

HAW HAW HA

What the---

ZIP

SIT--- STAY--- Bad Doggy!!!

CLOMP

HEY!

WHOA!
SNAP

HEEELLLLP

nice doggY!
SpLasH
OK, You can stop humming now.

SUPER DIAPER BABY

Chapter 4
HOORAY FOR DIAPER DOG

So Danger Dog Flew Billy back to his parents' house.

What if we make him wear a diaper?

Hmmm--- I guess that will be O.K.

And so Danger Dog changed his name to "Diaper Dog"...
Tee-Hee.
Doggy needs blankie.
Here is an extra Blanket.

... And a new crime-fighting duo was born.

BUT....
Meanwhile, at the Nuclear Power Plant, something terrible was happening to Deputy Doo-Doo.
Don't call me That!

The nuclear Radiation was making his body grow...

... and Grow...

... and grow...

... until suddenly...

I'm GonnA get You, Super Diaper Baby...
...and your Little DOG, too!
You know, I've seen People step on poo Before, but Ive never seen poo step on people!
Yeah, Life is Funny that way.

meanwhile, at the Hoskinses' House...
I will get DesserT.
KIBBLES

Look up in the sky--- It's A Turd!
It's A Plane!

... No, wait. You're Right... It's A turd.
KIBBLES

And so with Light-ning speed, our heroes Tied on their blankies.

And off they Flew.

me punch Poopy man.

No! Wait!

Don't Touch him! He has absorbed all the nuclear radiation from that Power plant.

You'll get mutated!

How we fight him?
I'm thinking, I'm thinking...
CRACK

missed us!
zip
zip
That was close!
SWISH

Hey! I've got it!!!

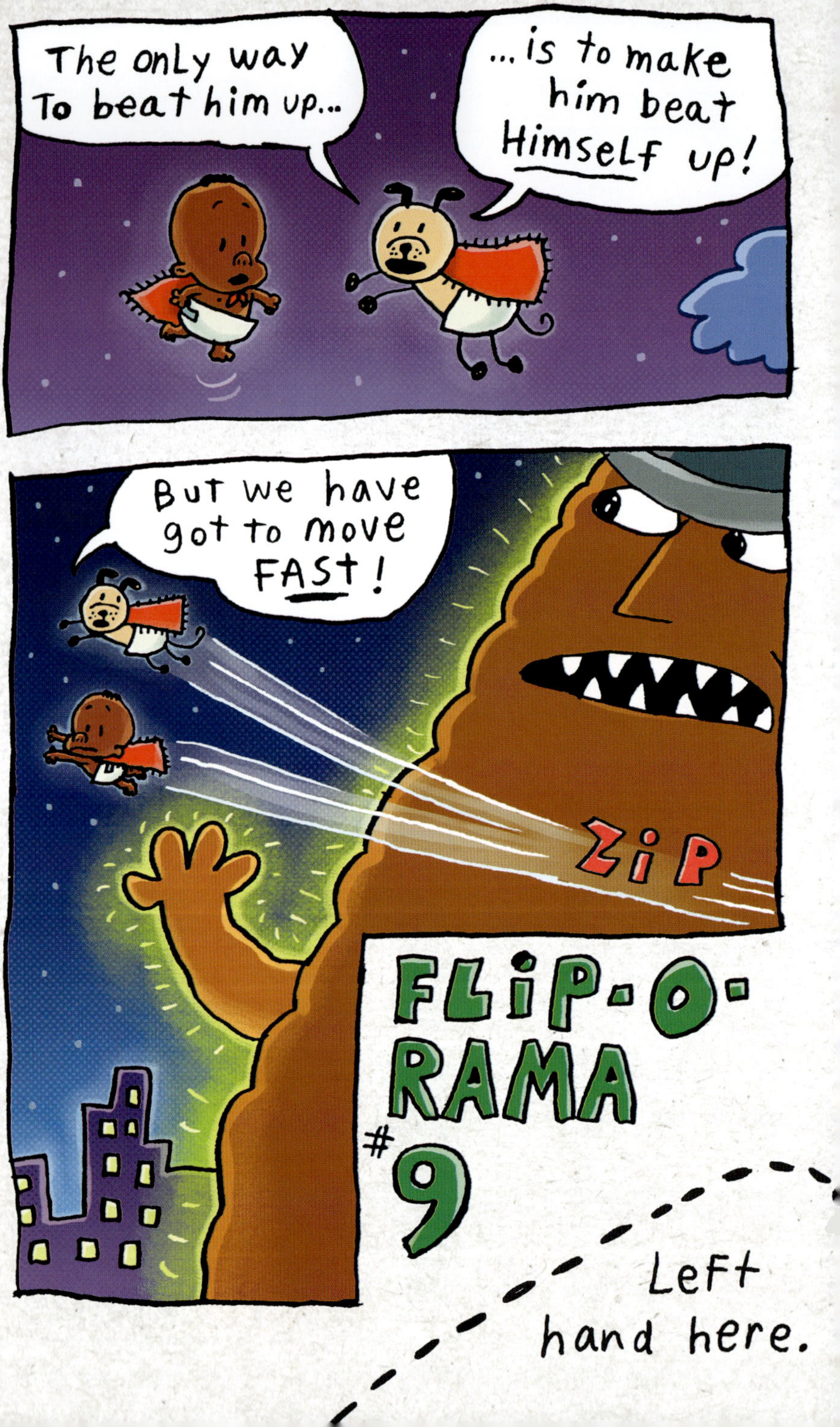

But we have got to move FAST!

ZiP

FLiP-O-RAMA #9

Left hand here.

"Poopy-Puncher"

"Poopy-Puncher"

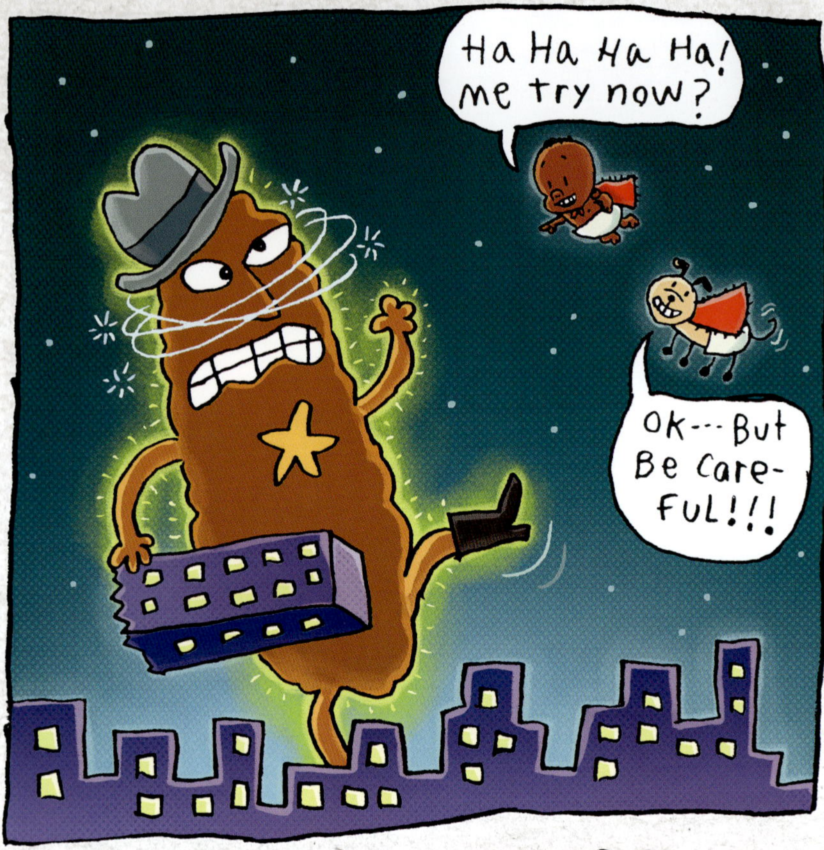

Ha Ha Ha Ha! me try now?

Ok--- But Be care-ful!!!

FLIP-O-RAMA #10

Left hand here.

Head Banger Blues

Head Banger Blues

Bob's Toilet Paper Co.

Sorry, BoB.
CRAK
BoB's ToiLeT Paper Co.
HeY!

FLIP-O-RAMA #11

Left hand here.

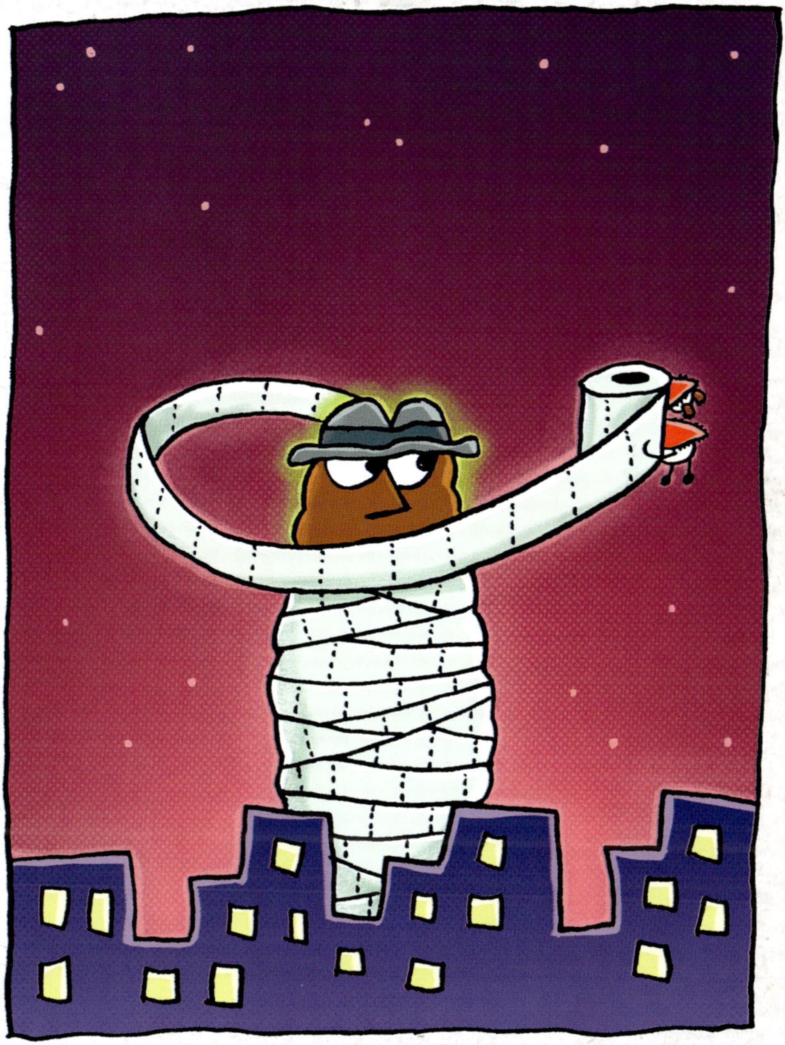

Around and Around
they went

Around and Around
they went

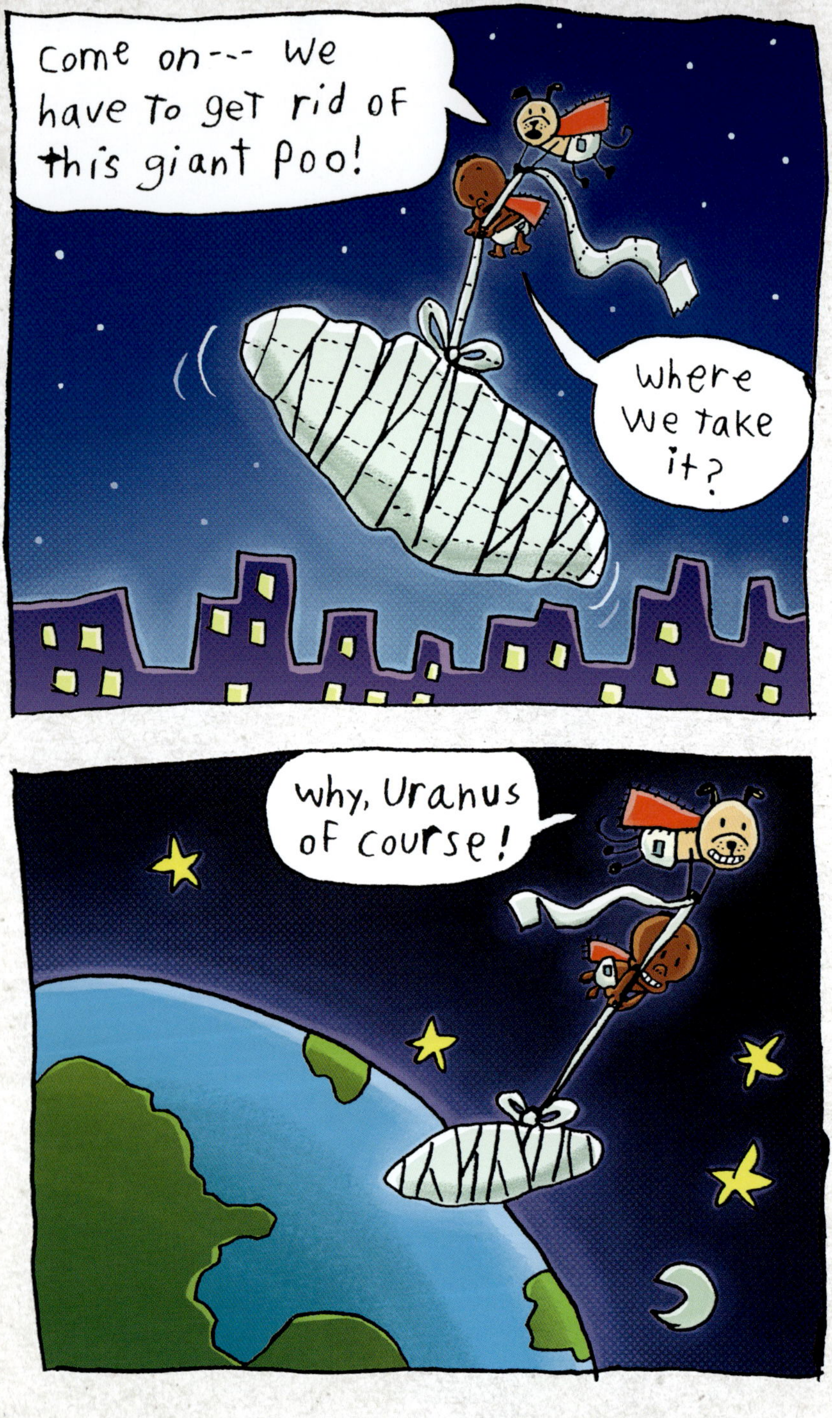

Come on--- we have to get rid of this giant poo!

Where we take it?

SUPER DIAPER BABY

CHAPTER 5
Happily Ever After

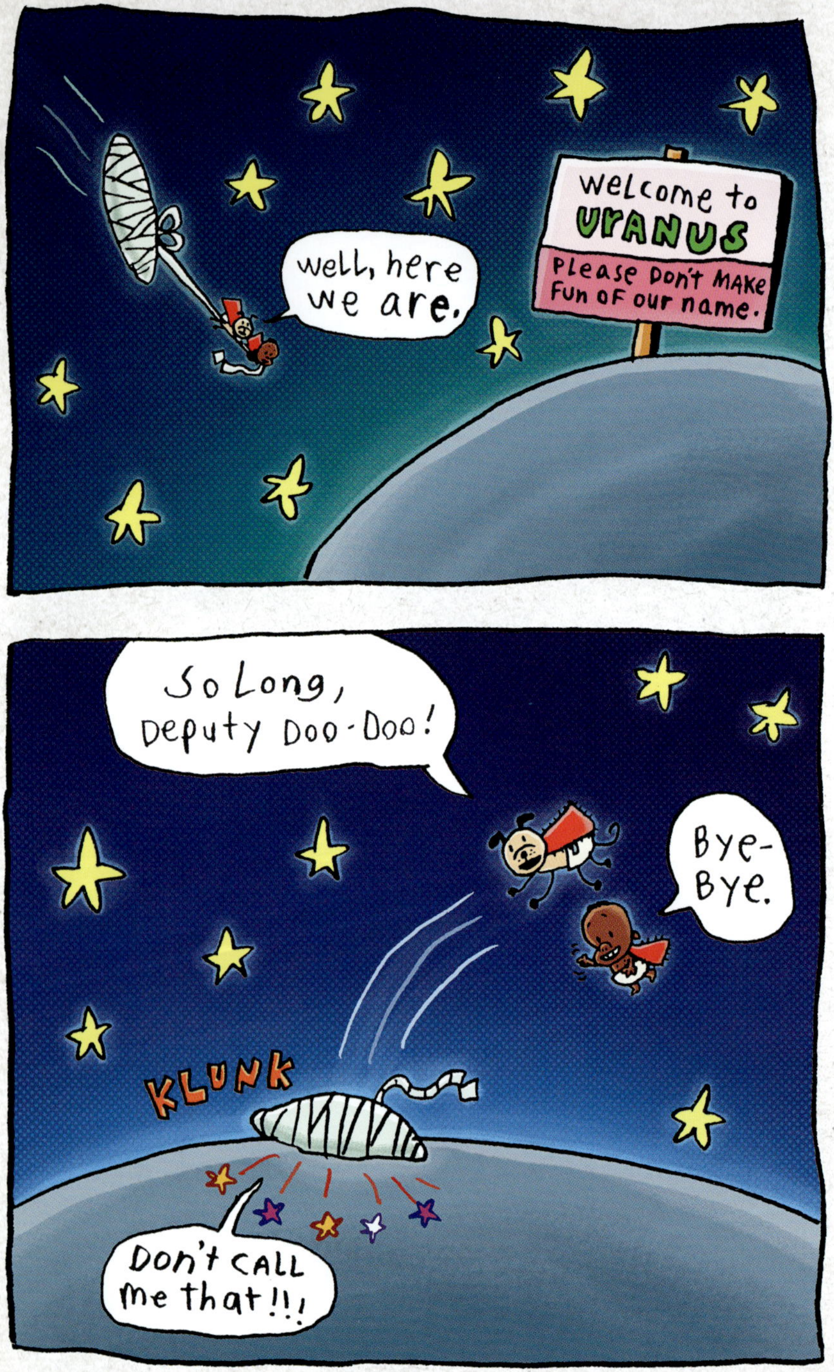

So Long, Deputy Doo-Doo!

Bye-Bye.

KLUNK

Don't CALL me that!!!

on their way back, our Heroes stopped at mars for some refreshments.
STARB
man, these Places are everywhere!

Can I help you?
Yeah, I'LL take a Large water... and a Juice box for the Kid.
me Like Juice box.

New Alien SuperPower Juice
Gives You super-powers!
Super-Power Juice
will there be any-thing else, sir?
Hmmm...

Why you buy SuperPower Juice?
I've got to make things right on earth!
STARBUTTS

EArth

Ye olde Underwear CLEANERS
Super-Heroes welcome

CRASH

Super-Power Juice
Drink up, bub!
Ha Ha-Underwear!

KA·POW
cover your eyes, Kid!

I Got my Superpowers Back! You were a good doggy after all!!!
Yeah, well... whatre ya gonna do?

The LAST FLIP-O-RAMA

Left hand here.

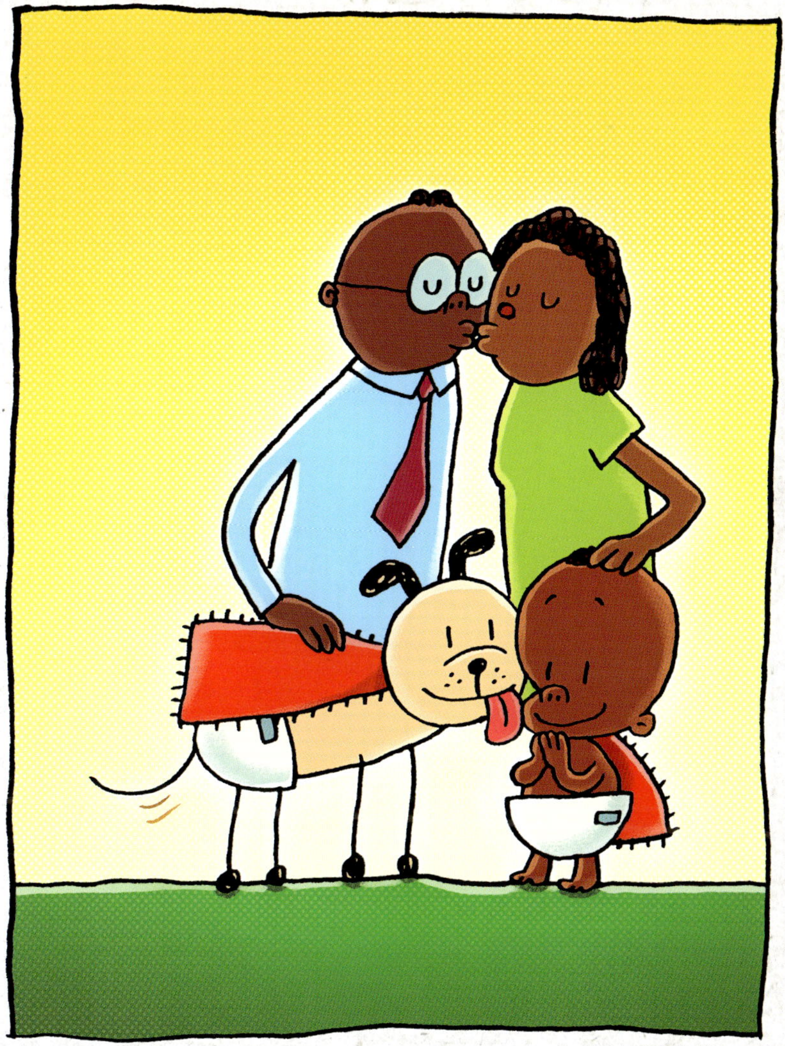

And they all Lived Happily ever After

Right Thumb here.

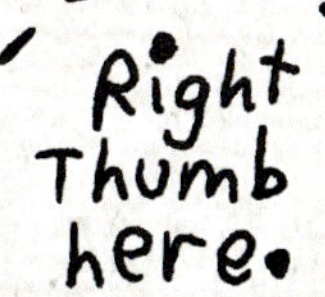

And they all Lived Happily ever After

THE

END

How 2 Draw Super Diaper Baby

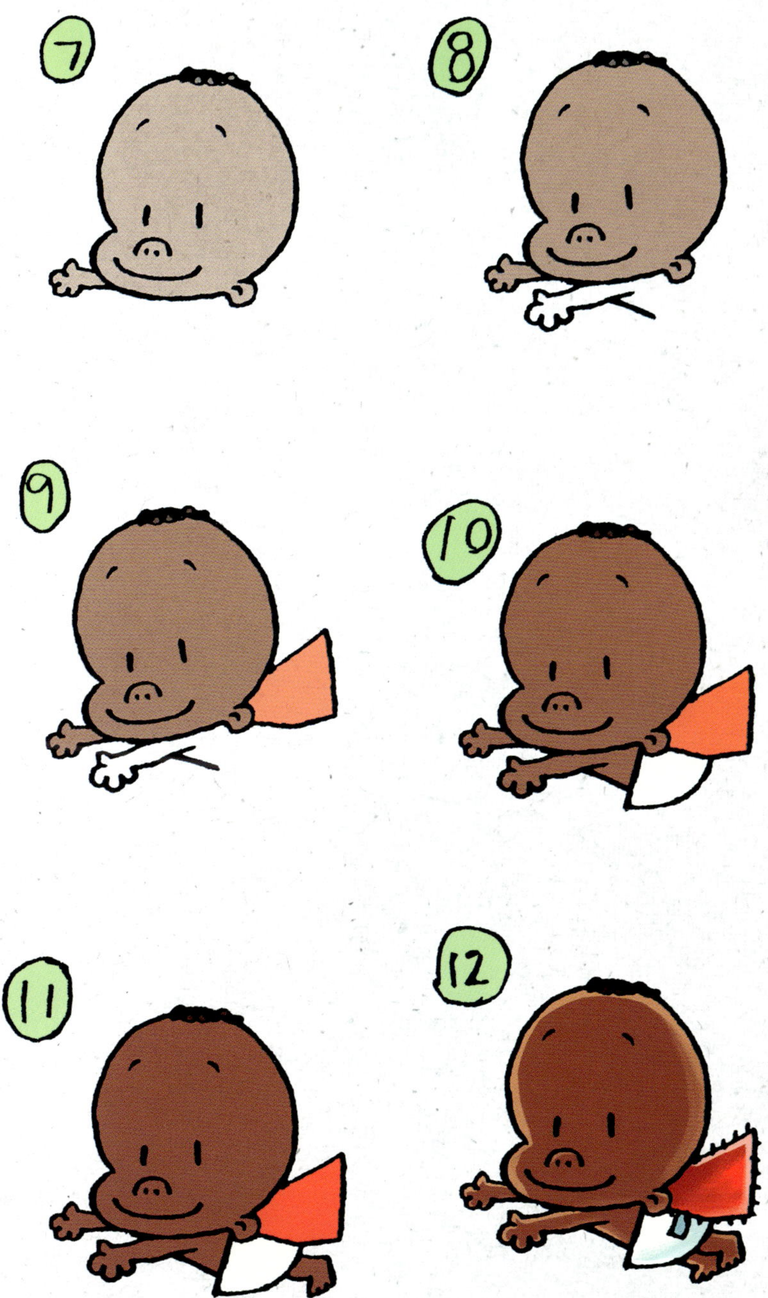
7
8
9
10
11
12

How 2 Draw Diaper Dog

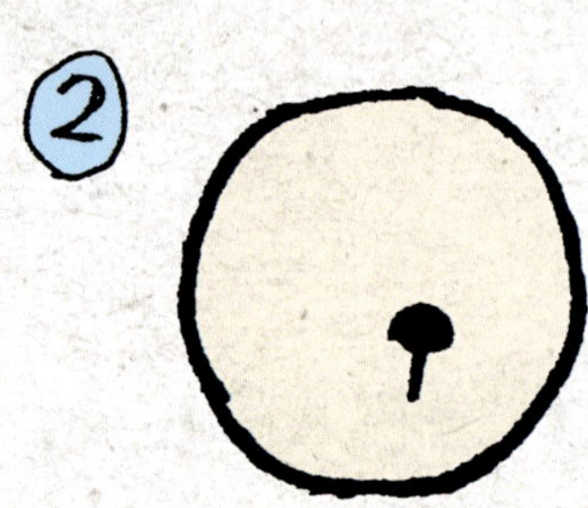

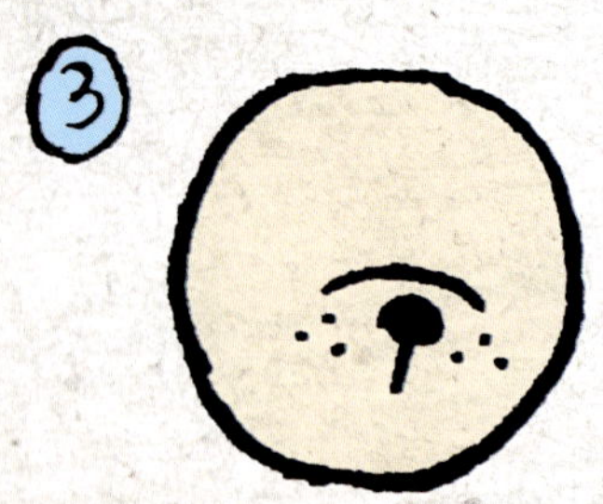

7

8

9

10

11

12

How 2 Draw Deputy Doo-Doo

1

2

3

4

5

6

7

8

9

10

11

12

HOW 2 DRAW
The Robo-Ant 2000

9

10

11

12

13

14

About the Author and Illustrator

GEORGE BEARD (age 9¾)

is the co-creator of such wonderful comic book characters as Captain Underpants, Timmy the Talking Toilet, and The Amazing Cow Lady.

Besides making comics, George enjoys skateboarding, watching TV, playing video games, pulling pranks, and saving the world. His favorite food is chocolate chip cookies.

George lives with his mom and dad and his two cats, Porky and Buckwheat. He is currently a fourth grader at Jerome Horwitz Elementary School in Piqua, Ohio.

HAROLD HUTCHINS (age 10)

has co-written and illustrated more than thirty comic books with his best pal (and next-door neighbor), George Beard.

When he is not making comics, Harold can usually be found drawing or reading comics. He also enjoys skateboarding, playing video games, and watching Japanese monster movies. His favorite food is gum.

Harold lives with his mom and his little sister, Heidi. He has five goldfish named Moe, Larry, Curly, Dr. Howard, and SuperFang.

Read on for the behind-the-scenes story about the making of this book, pages from Dav Pilkey's sketchbook, and more!

THE STORY BEHIND THE STORY

In case you didn't know, this book was really written by George and Harold's alter ego — me! My name is Dav Pilkey. That's me below.

George and Harold are very real characters to me. I based both of them on myself when I was a kid. So when I started working on this book, I needed to "become" George and Harold. In my imagination, I stopped being me, and sort of let them take over. I let them create the story they wanted, without worrying about spelling, or grammar, or moralistic plots that would please adults. (For this edition, the spelling and grammar mistakes were corrected.)

I was also inspired by the homemade comic books I receive from kids every day. Their comics sometimes contain misspelled words and usually have bad guys who are disgusting in one way or another.

But the amazing thing is that these comics are all made voluntarily. Nobody forces those kids to make comic books. They just do it for fun. And there's always something wonderful about that kind of unprompted creativity. I really tried to capture some of that energy in this book.

PART 1: THE INSPIRATION

When I was making *Captain Underpants and the Wrath of the Wicked Wedgie Woman* (which contains three comics by George and Harold), I began to imagine how much fun it would be to do an entire book of comics.

At first, I wanted to do a collection of short, unrelated comic stories by George and Harold. I wrote down a bunch of ideas and titles. But Super Diaper Baby didn't really appear until I began to draw sketches. This sketch was the beginning of everything. I liked the way the baby looked so much that I immediately decided to do a whole book about him.

PART 2: THE SKETCHES

When I first begin to work out a story (which I usually do in my head), it helps me to have visual references. So I like to draw sketches of the main characters and write down who they are and what role they will play in the story.

Here are my first character sketch sheets:

I KEEEL YOU!
ALL NEW
ALL COMICS
Flip-O-RAMA in every chapter!
ALL LAFFS
Dude, Trust me.
You Reek!
When the world's Greatest superhero, Captain Underpants, loses all of his powers, it's up to ONE
But who will save the world?
me will
Super Draper Baby
Billy Hoskins
Diaper DOG
Deputy Doo-Doo
Deputy Dangerous

PART 3: FIGURING OUT THE STORY

Usually, I find it helpful to make notes on a story BEFORE I write it. The next two pages are from an early draft.

You'll notice that these pages have pictures in the margins.

I find that it's helpful to draw while I write, because I often get good ideas from my sketches.

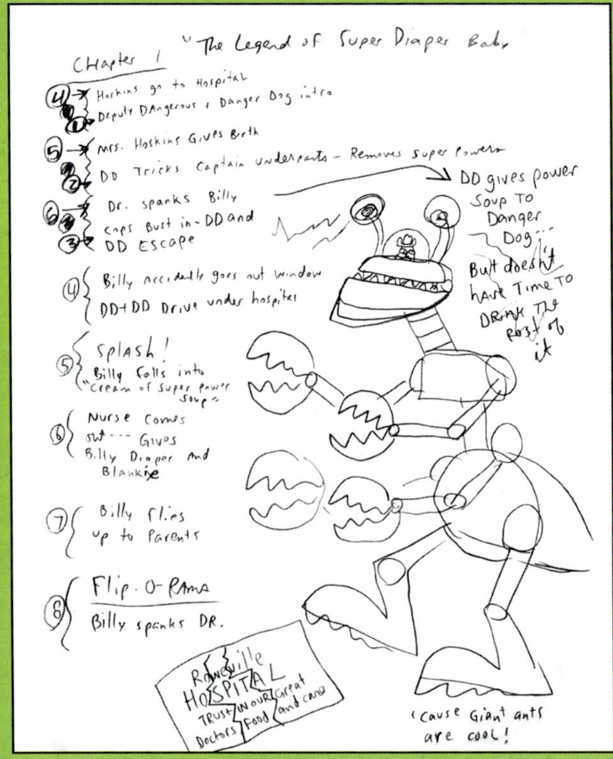

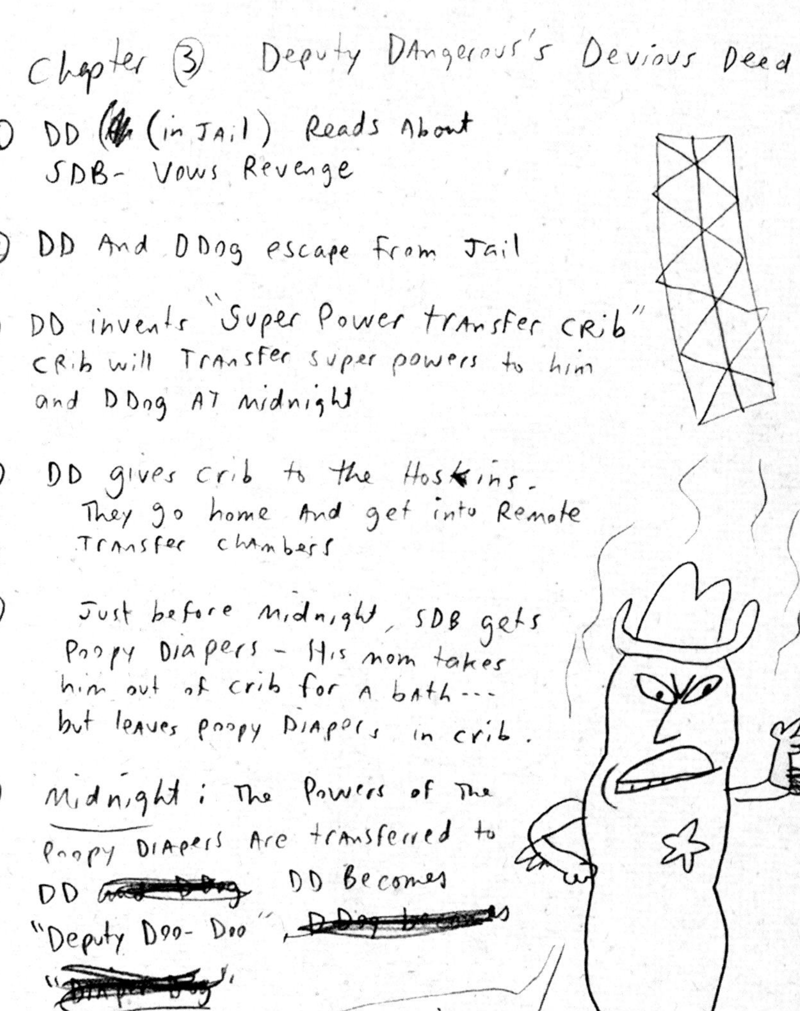

Chapter ③ Deputy DAngerous's Devious Deed

① DD (in JAil) Reads About SDB- Vows Revenge

② DD And DDog escape from Jail

③ DD invents "Super Power transfer cRib" cRib will TrAnsfer super powers to him and DDog AT midnight

④ DD gives crib to the Hoskins. They go home And get into Remote TrAnsfer chAmbers

⑤ Just before midnight, SDB gets Poopy DiApers - His mom takes him out of crib for A bath--- but leaves poopy DiApers in crib.

⑥ Midnight: The Powers of The Poopy DiApers Are transferred to DD. DD Becomes "Deputy Doo-Doo",

⑦ "I'll get even with Super DiAper BAby if it's the LAst thing I Do!"

8 flip o RAmA?

PART 4:
THE THUMBNAILS

I created this book in a different way from most of my other books because the story and art were more important than the writing. In fact, I didn't even write the text for this book until I had figured out where the drawings were going to go.

To do this, I created thumbnails, which are like a map of the book. They show an illustrator all of the pages of a book at once. Each box on the next page represents a page in the book. The sketches inside each little box helped me to decide how much room I had to put words on each page.

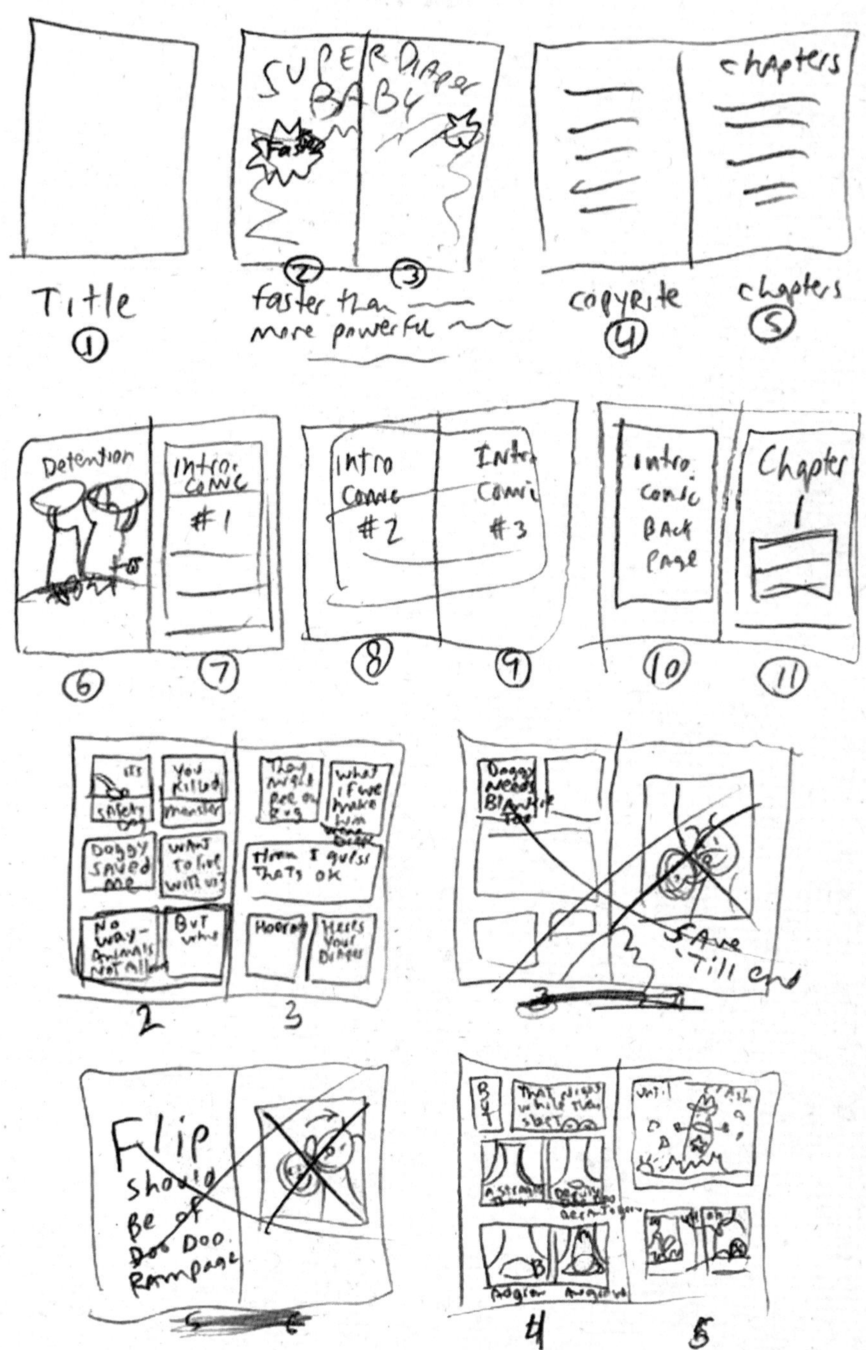
SUPER DIAPER BABY
Title
faster than
more powerful
copyrite
chapters
Detention
Intro comic #1
Intro comic #2
Intro comic #3
Intro comic BACK page
Chapter 1
You killed monster
Doggy saved me
No way—Animals not allowed
But who
What if we make him
Hmm I guess thats ok
Hooray
Heres your Diaper
Doggy needs blankie too
SAVE 'Till end
Flip should be of Doo Doo Rampage
That night while they slept

PART 5: THE STORYBOARDS

After the thumbnails were completed, I made a more detailed rough draft. These drawings are called storyboards. This is where I did most of the work on the book. If you look closely at the next group of pictures, you'll see that I was still trying to figure out parts of the story at this stage.

There are many differences between what appears in the storyboards and what ended up in the book.

Well What
Do you Think of My Robo Ant 2000?
Can I call you "Deputy Doo-Doo" from now on?
AAAUGH
You won't Be LAughing So Hard After I destroy The world!
3

CRASH
Tee Hee
Hey, wait up
SECRE
LABRA
15%
So The Robo Ant 2000 set out on An evil RAmpAge
come with me if you want Kibbles!
mkay
UH oh
Thump
4

ZAP
HA HA
Hi-YAH
CRACK
SPIT IN The food
5

Our Pizzas Are made with fresh Cheese
Our workers cut the
Our pizzas are made with
CRACK
grass clippings
Cheese
CRACK
Switchie Switchie
Hey!
Pizzas are made w/ grass clippings
Our workers cut the Cheese
6

PART 6: THE EDITING

Before I show any of this to my editor, I read through it all and cut out anything that is unnecessary.

I decided to drop several panels from these storyboards because I felt that they slowed down the pace of the story.

PART 7:
THE COVER

Then it was time to draw the cover.

Here is a pencil sketch:

GET READING W

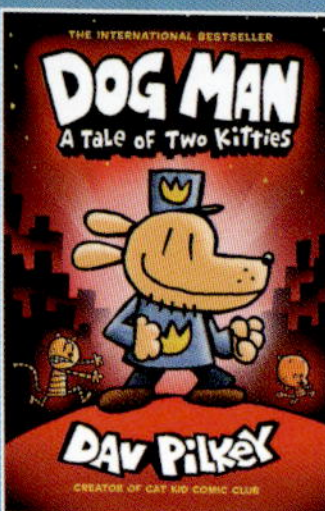

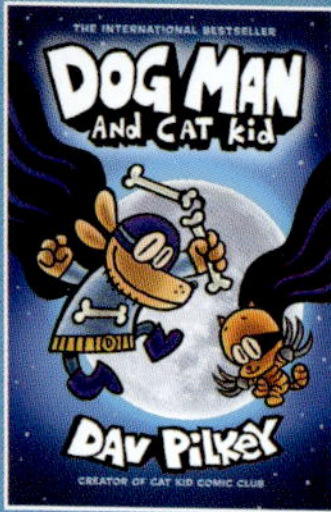

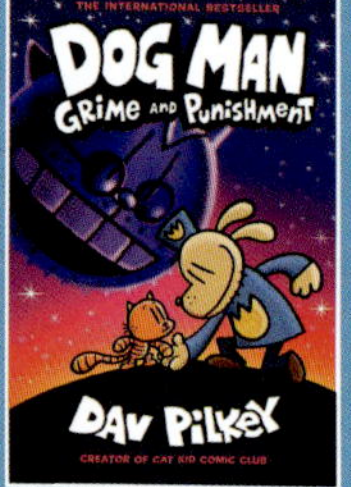

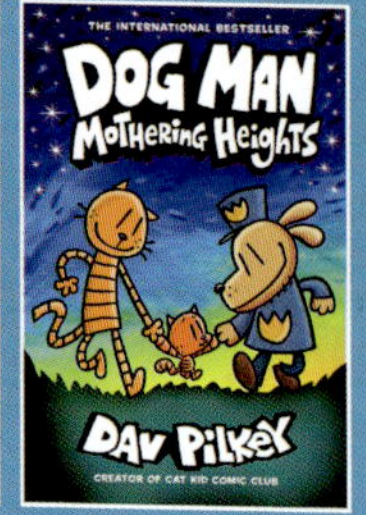

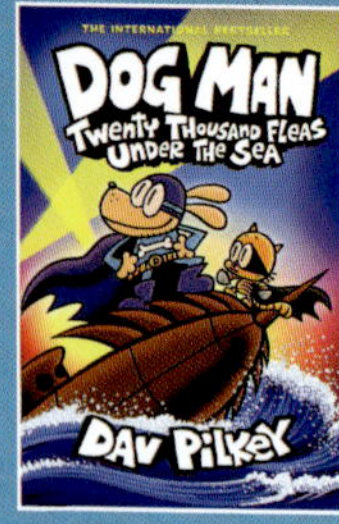

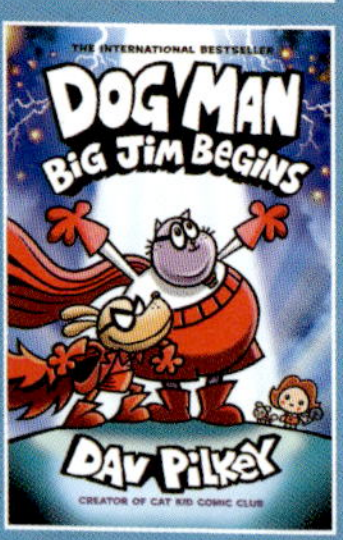

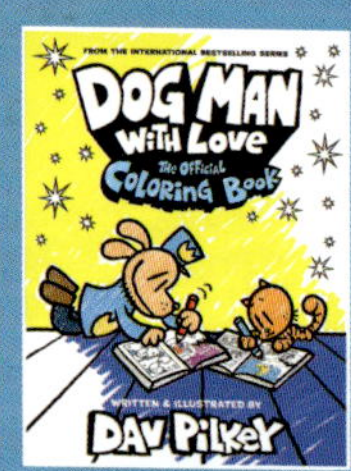

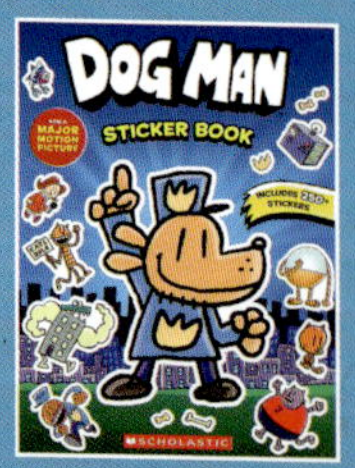

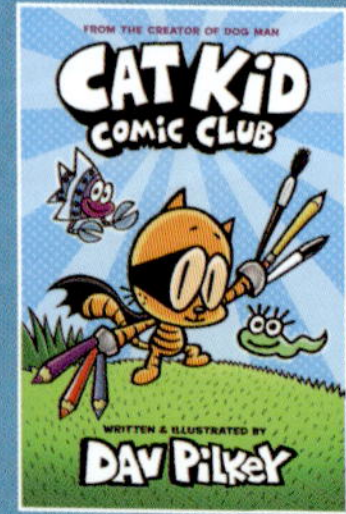

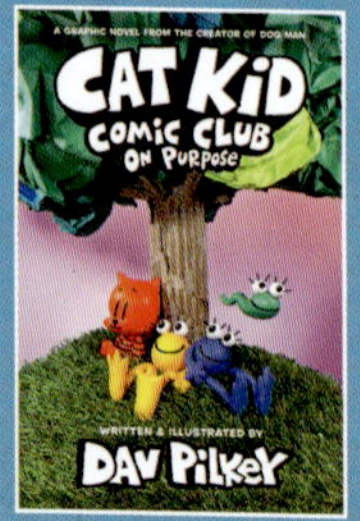

★ "Irreverent, laugh-out-loud funny, and . . . downright moving."
— Publishers Weekly, starred review

...TH DAV PILKEY!

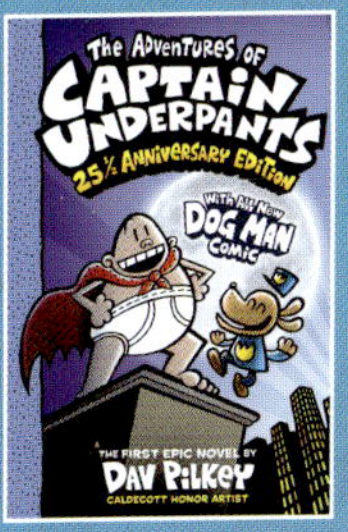

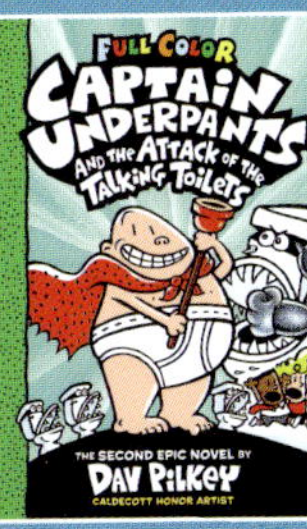

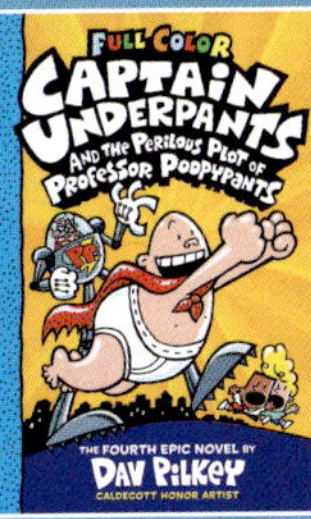

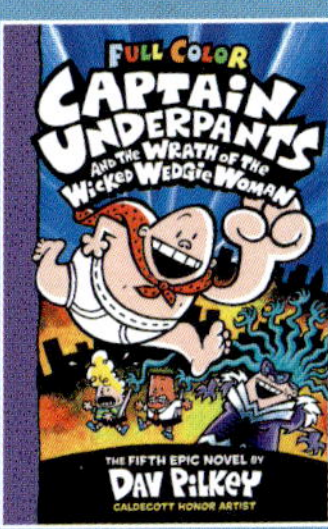

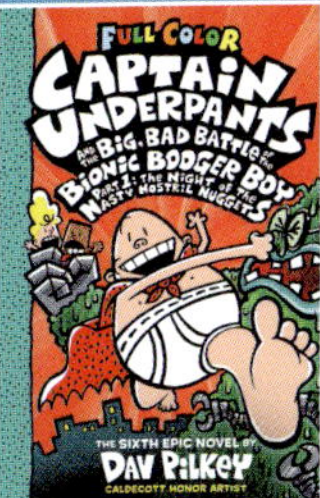

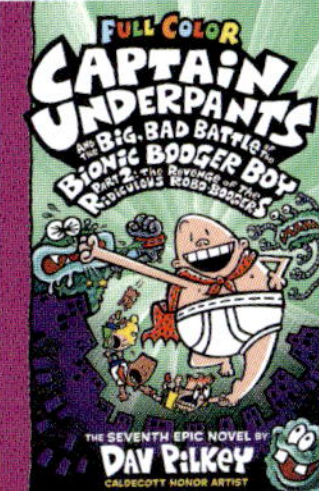

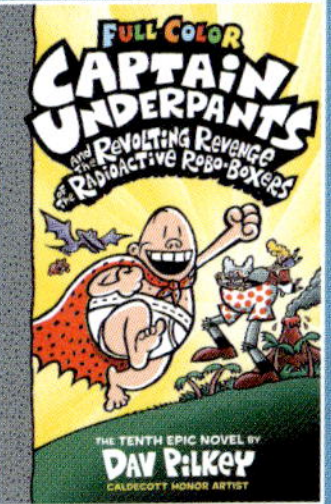

The epic musical adventure is now available from Broadway Records!

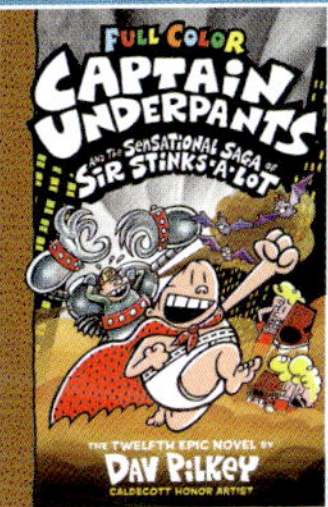

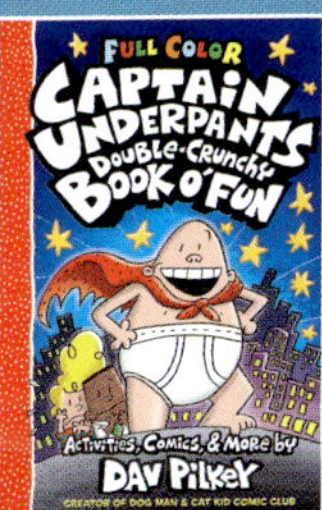

Go to PlanetPilkey.com to join Dav Pilkey's Epic Comic Club, read chapters, watch videos, and make comics!

About the Author-Illustrator

When Dav Pilkey was a kid, he was diagnosed with ADHD and dyslexia. Dav was so disruptive in class that his teachers made him sit out in the hallway every day. Luckily, Dav loved to draw and make up stories. He spent his time in the hallway creating his own original comic books — the very first adventures of Dog Man and Captain Underpants.

In the second grade, Dav's teacher ripped up his comics and told him he couldn't spend the rest of his life making silly books.

Fortunately, Dav was not a very good listener.